AFTERMATH

Aftermath

NIKKI MERRIMAN

CPR Publishing

Copyright © 2022 by Nikki Merriman

All rights reserved. No part of this book may be reproduced in any manner whatsoever without written permission except in the case of brief quotations embodied in critical articles and reviews.

First Printing, 2022

For Amanda, my actual soulmate here on earth. I couldn't do anything in this life without you by my side. Thank you for giving me your strength and your grace when I can't manage to find my own. Thank you for being an absolute angel- my absolute angel.

PREFACE

What do you do when you wake up one morning, and your life is turned inside out? How do you process it? What's the first thing you do? What do you do when you find out that everything you thought you knew and were building your life around was a lie- and not a small one? Unfortunately, in late summer 2022, that became my reality when I opened my phone to a text from my long-time girlfriend ending our relationship. Over the weeks that followed, the truth that came out would blow my mind. Not only had she cheated multiple times throughout the beginning of our relationship (that we'd chosen to work through and stay together through), she'd actually met another woman 11 years younger than her only about a month earlier, built a relationship with her behind my back, and actually ended up moving this other woman and her kid into her house right under my nose a week BEFORE she broke up with me. All within approximately a month. I'm not easily made speechless, but discovering this information definitely did the trick. At first I'd just been told she left me because she didn't want to be in a relationship at all, then eventually I was told it was for another woman; the full truth came out in pieces over the course of about a month. Needless to say, I was far from okay. To say I was hurting was a gross understatement.

However, as all this was coming to light, as I was dealing with this massive level of hurt and betrayal, something beautiful was unfolding. I'd out of the blue reconnected with someone with whom I'd agreed to go on a date and, well, here I am writing a book. Suddenly, there were two sides of my life: the dark, stormy, hurt and betrayed side that I'd come to know all too well, but now there was also this peaceful side that came with this seemingly odd sense of security and belonging that I could just melt into after a long day. An honest, patient, and graceful side. A side that embraced me as I was. How was it possible that these two sides of my life could exist on the same plane? How was this person seeing the woman behind the wall I'd built? How could I be writing both parts of this book at the same time?

"Aftermath" isn't the long, drawn out, 200-page book you've probably come to expect from me by now. It wasn't written over the span of a year to a year and a half. It doesn't encompass my many life experiences. It's short, it's pinpoint focused, and it only follows a couple months of my life. It's the light and the dark, the good and the bad, the calm and the storm, and it's both sides of a double-edged sword. It's not my typical body of work- it's a healing project for me- but I hope you'll embrace it just as openly.

THE BREAKING

I need to promise myself
that this book will be
the last time
I let you let me down

Let me tell you
the story of my heart-

It begins and ends
with her

"I don't want to be someone you write about"

Darling, don't you know?

You were so much more
than just words on a page-
you were love
and light
and hope in the darkest of days.

But all it came down to
was this.

Was a still beating heart
ripped from my bleeding chest
with lying, cheating hands-
hands that did not care to know
what they held
when they held that heart

I cannot keep my promise
not to write about you-

After all,
you were my favorite muse

I guess our forevers had very different meanings;

I meant it when I said
hello,
and you meant it when you said
goodbye

I looked for you
in every crowded room-
your brown eyes,
your long, dark hair,
your contagious smile.

I had no idea
you were looking for her.

My god,
I loved you with everything in me
(and then some)

But I couldn't love you enough
to stop you from loving her more

I could've
(and would've)
loved you forever

If you only knew
how to let yourself be loved

It will take everything in me
to forget
even the way you held my hand

They ask me how I am,
as if bombs were not dropping around me,
as if my world had not been turned upside down,
as if my feet were still on solid ground.

They ask me how I am,
as if you were still here

—I'm fine

And oh,
the goddamn nerve of you
to tell me you loved me

Someday,
when the new wears off
and the shine goes dull,

you'll think of me.

One day,
I won't cry over you anymore.

Until then,
these tears will fall
like rain-
let them.

Suddenly,
life moved in slow motion
as you left
as you lied
as you said there was someone else

Suddenly,
I was trying to breathe underwater,
trying to swim against the tide
that was carrying you away

—drowning

Tell me this-

Who do you think you are?

To leave these scars and
run,
not turning back for so much as an
apology

You can't blame this one
on the skeletons in your closet

Maybe you were never actually mine
(maybe you were)
but the way I loved you said otherwise
(maybe I always will)

Simply put,
this isn't the way
I wanted to love you forever

How was I supposed to know?
That every time you looked at me,
you saw her

Someday,
this will be but a moment in time
but for now,
I cannot escape
the moment you left
the moment you lied
the moment you wouldn't even look me in the eye

I'm not sure what scares me more:
knowing I don't have you,
or not knowing who I am without you

I'm still adjusting to writing about you
like this.

I've always written about you
with so much love
that the heartbreak that now surrounds your words
seems too foreign
to even be real

How was I to know
that you were too good to be true?

When you left
you took a part of me
that will never return

I will not go quietly
out the door
that you slammed in my face

—what do you expect from an author

You were so careful not to cut yourself
on the fragments of the heart you broke
that you never even considered
how deeply they cut into me

Forever too much,
but never enough-

how do I balance
on the edge of this sword?

It's too late
for you to hear
the words I left unsaid

Tell me
what is left
for me to defend?

This barren desert
you've left me standing in
is hardly it

I'll be forever grasping at memories
for the last time
I saw your face

All I'll ever be to you
is a bump in the road,

but all you'll ever be to me
is everything

What it came down to
was this:

We were a one sided
second chance
fight... for what?

—I've always been the fighter

They say that
healing isn't linear.

They don't warn you
that it's a goddamn
rollercoaster

—I want off this ride

I guess I tried
too desperately
to change our ending
(I've always been a little too hopeful)

You are not something
I ever thought
I'd have to learn how to survive

Your silence screams louder
than your
"I love you"
ever did

Somewhere in your lies
we lost all our magic
(magic is just an illusion, anyway)
(maybe this time it was real)

There is love
there is loss
and then there is you–

the deadliest combination
of the two

Today,
I say goodbye
to the love engraved in my bones.

Today,
I say goodbye to us.

Who you are
is written in my heart,
on my soul.

I think what I'm trying to say
is I don't know how not to love you

In the middle of the night
when she's asleep
and the world is still,
I can't help but wonder
(hope)
if your mind wanders back to
us

You did not care
when you left me standing
in the middle of ashes that have yet to fully
settle;
what will I find when they do?
(how far gone will you be?)

You'll always find
me
haunting you
at the bottom of your midnight bottle

The moment I knew
you loved her more,
my heart broke into pieces so
s h a r p
my soul bled

Tell me how to learn
to do life without you-
without the love
I let my soul melt into

I see your face
every time I close my eyes.

I know we'll meet again
in every midnight dream,
but my heart breaks all over again
with every sunrise
when you're not there beside me

You lit a match
in the form of her
and burned to the ground
the home I built in you

I will not emerge from your fires
unscathed,
but have you ever seen a phoenix?
(if I emerge at all)
(someday I will)

She is a hurricane
(category 5)
ripping up the coast
destroying everything in her path
showing no signs of stopping.

But my god,
the worst storms
always have the most
beautiful
(brown)
eyes

THE AFTERMATH

This is hope in its rawest form.
This is
love
and this is
faith
and this is the light of peace at the end of the tunnel,
all wrapped up in one
wonderful
blue eyed package

Your patience and your grace
will be what pulls me through this

I'm not used to someone so gentle with me;
so kind with his words,
so patient with his heart,
so honest with his soul

—a tragedy

Kiss me darling
until I'm yours
(and then never stop)

Here
wrapped up in your arms
I can feel the pieces of my soul being cemented back together
with the most beautiful gold

What a heartbreaking thing it is,
to have to learn all over again
how to be loved.

What a wonderful thing,
to be learning it from you.

I think you might be my favorite
unanswered prayer

And you caught me off guard
when I braced myself,
and you didn't leave

I am a new me;
we will both learn to love her
at the same time

Maybe I could get used to
writing about love again
(maybe I could get used to you)

Baptize me
in the river of your soul

One look from you
is all it took
for my world to flash
the most glorious shade of blue

—I always had a thing for blue eyes

The nights aren't quite as dark
wrapped up here in your arms

It takes a special kind of person
to quiet the
war zone
inside of my heart
(the bombs are dropping)
(you're waving the white flag)

I'm still learning to write
like this again
but for you,
I'll keep writing

Slow down-
I want tonight to last
just a little while longer

I'll always dance the night away
with you.

Until my legs give out,
until my knees buckle beneath me,
until my ankles can't stand,
I'll dance with you

I could find a home
in this
(fragile)
hope
you've built around me

Pull me close,
wrap me up in you,
and feel me come undone at your touch

You
are my favorite act of
bravery

I cannot wait to memorize
every inch
of who you are

—body and soul

Somewhere between
your blue eyes
and the way you say my name,
I fell so much harder for you
than I ever planned
(and I'm not stopping)

There are so many things
I want to say to you,
but instead I'll kiss you goodnight
and hope my voice finds the courage
in the morning

I can't help but fall
a little harder for you
with every golden sunrise

Somewhere between the
late nights
and
early mornings,
I got lucky enough
to call you mine

Take my hand
and let's make the most
out of this
miracle
we've been given

—second chances

Little did I know
that you were a world of
peace
waiting just around the corner
from a pile of
ashes
and dust
and sharp heart fragments

"Pick your battles,"
they say.

But let me tell you,
I will choose every day
to fight tooth and nail
to break down
every
single
wall
you've built around yourself

Here's me,
heart on my sleeve
hope in my heart
light in my eyes
love in my soul.

Here's me,
next to you.

It's okay if heights aren't your thing-
jump anyway
(we're all afraid of something)
(I'll catch you)

I never was a gambler,
but I'll make you one bet-

I'll bet you
your heart
that I'll change your life

—shake on it

You press your forehead to mine,
and time stops
and the world swirls around us
and I just want to hold onto this moment
a little (a lot) tighter

You're the only person
who can make an empty dancefloor
in the middle of a mansion
surrounded by staring strangers
feel like the only place in the world
I want to be

You took one look
at the walls I'd built
and somehow knew
there was a human behind them worth reaching

I can't promise you
that you'll never fall
never fail
never hit the ground.

But I can promise
that I'll sit beside you,
bandage your skinned knees,
and sit with you
until you're ready to get back up
(I'll always pull you back up)

I look at you
from across the room
and suddenly I don't know
that I've ever known peace
until this moment

Tell me your deepest and your darkest;
your soul is safe
with me and the night

You took my hand
as you asked me to dance,
and little did I know
in that moment
that my heart would no longer
be my own

I'll fall for you
over
and over
and over again-
all you have to do is ask

To put it simply,
you are everything
I didn't know I needed
in this world

Maybe this time,
these butterflies
aren't a warning

Our story started
not too late
but right on time;

let's write these next pages
together

Our whole world
could change
with just one kiss

I'll be thankful everyday
for this second chance
to explore this
electric
connection between us

I'm so many things,
but
yours
might be my new favorite

One look from you
knows how to quiet
the chaos in my heart

You're my favorite
midnight bedroom slow dance,

my favorite
lazy good morning kiss,

and my favorite
everything in between

It's as if my soul met yours
and whispered to my heart,
"it's okay to beat again"

—safe

My favorite thing about sunsets
is knowing you'll be right there
next to me
when the sun comes back up in the morning

And when the night is spent
and the drinks are gone,
I promise to always dance
the very last dance
with you

—Never Stop, SafetySuit

Dear lord,
don't let me start
missing her now

Nikki is a runner, dancer, model, and traumatic brain injury survivor from the Chicagoland area. When she isn't writing, she enjoys painting, traveling, and spending time with her family and pets. More often than not, you can find her on the beach or near the water. There are few things she enjoys more than hearing from her readers; you can find her and more of her work on Instagram @nixwrites_.

www.ingramcontent.com/pod-product-compliance
Lightning Source LLC
Chambersburg PA
CBHW070434010526
44118CB00014B/2041